STEPHEN WARREN HEWITT

PURSUED by a Different World

An Encounter With The Heart's Desires

A COLLECTION OF RHYTHMIC POETRY

Pursued by a Different World: An Encounter With The Heart's Desire

ISBN-13: 978-0-6151-3468-0

ISBN-10: 0-615-13468-8

Printed in the United States of America.

Cover design: Christine and Stephen Hewitt

Interior images: © 2006 JupiterImages Corporation and

© Nova Development Corporation

Stephen Hewitt contact information

Email: s_hewitt@bellsouth.net

CONTENTS

ACKNOWLEDGEMENTS

I would like to express my loyalty and special love for a lovely and enduring lady, my wife Christy. It would be worth it if I had written this book solely for her. Her beautiful responses to my poetry took me by poetic surprise. Christy's amazing patience and help, while I attempted to teach myself, made it possible for me to pursue poetic language in a context of quiet and calm. She, on the other hand, works in a fast-paced, business setting that can drain the human spirit if not replenished. It is for this replenishing that I write.

I thank my mother and father also for their undying patience while I pursued my adventure. As a young boy they provided me a family that gave me the needed instincts to explore and experience some amazingly good things in this life including my brother, sister and a few neat pets.

I call attention to all the times I spent admiring the beautiful outdoors. These times formed deep channels in my person and without them I would be a much different and lesser human being.

ABOUT THE AUTHOR

If you've ever wanted to meet someone who pursues the best of desire, then I suggest Stephen Hewitt is that person. At six years old Steve already showed the sensitivity of an artist. Unfortunately, his talent remained hidden until he finished seminary. His aesthetic desire arose in things like his first garden, his love of music including playing the piano and being a part-time DJ, and a *Starship* he made from *Kentucky Fried Chicken* buckets. But it is his keen emotional awareness of language coupled with his thirst for Beauty and Goodness that leads Steve to take poetry seriously. A fundamental tenant present in Steve's poetry is that Good is more mysterious and greater than evil.

Steve's time growing up in local churches, then college and seminary led him to reconsider the sound of human discourse. Something about it wasn't right. The sound of mystery such as that displayed in *The Lord of the Rings* seemed to disappear in the hands of politicians, theologians, and pastors. He heard language consistently send out a cry for help because it could no longer inspire and heal the wounded heart. Dead language permeates corporate speak, anesthetizing average people if they are not careful. Academia revels in flat discourse while its poets slowly drink and spread the poison. The Romantics were driven to rediscover language and experience, so it is with this poet. Some of Steve's favorite poets include Blake, Cowper, Smart, Traherne, Vaughan, and Wordsworth.

This incredibly different, but enriching world pursues Steve as he enjoys life in Zebulon, North Carolina, with his wife, Christy and their dog, AJ (a sable and white Sheltie) and their orange tabby cat, Rascal.

A Moment When the Soul Gazes

There is a moment when the soul gazes on its find,
a place for two hearts to share their minds,
a rhythm for each to feel its kind.

There is a someone wishing to read a human book,
a moon who needs the light of the sun's look,
a flower who needs the touch of a bee's work.

There is a love that needs the breath of fragrant air,
an evening that longs to present the stars aware,
a deer who runs the open field looking for thee there.

There is a wind longing to gentle blow,
a man desiring the gratitude of his betrothed,
a woman hoping for the satisfaction of her soul.

There is a hand wanting the guidance of a friend,
a mind hoping to overcome the darkened,
a song wanting to escape the heart's end.

There is a bird who dances in the magenta sky,
a pie shared at holiday times,
a pine listening to its needles' rhyme.

a moment where all this can be for thee,
a moment where all this can be for thee.

An Entirely Different World

Feel the subtle ripples
        form on the sandy beach
As the surf's imagination
        shapes and steadily sweeps.

Listen to the water
as she caresses the sand.
Feel the sand release
to her hands' demand.

See the gentle waves
        whisper "Come to me,"
While the grains
        entertain her lovely tease.

Touch the tiny granules
as they dance for her.
Remember the tender
rhythm as the night occurs.

Beautiful creativity,
        she refreshes the beach,
With excited moving
        specks within her reach.

Continued

Rhythm suggests a beauty
to pursue for thee.
Each wants an inspired
love like land and sea.

Under the moon's lure
continues a romantic swirl,
Waiting for someone to feel
this entirely different world.

When Light Discovers Light

Good evening, Mr. Moon,
We have conversed so many times.
Tonight, I'd like you to meet
My wife and gentle rhyme.

Mr. Moon, you and I know
Each other well and with friendly ease.
Thank you for sending your dovelike light
Through my tall and lovely trees.

You made it so easy
To enjoy the gentle and nightly breeze;
Divine beauty I could only feel
Tasting you upon the pleasant seas.

And while viewed through
The many places and so many sweet pines,
He illumined you to rise
And set his divinely poetic lines.

But before I forget to say,
While the angels play with singleness;
I'd like to thank you most of all
For bringing light to your caretaker's eminence.

Continued

You perform the moon so well,

    I simply wonder who taught thee your elegance.

I hope our friendship today can be the same

    For you and my mate's willingness.

She is special too

    Just like you, you see.

She opines with a light

    That touches sweetly me.

Watch With Me

Watch with me
the milky moon's duet with the morning star,
    the tender trills of a leaf's delicate descent,
    the delightful depths of a faithful kiss.

Watch with me
a carefree kitten's playful swirls,
    a musical mother's protective song,
    a laugh leaping from a jolly soul.

"Watch with me and sing." Says the one who enables me.

Watch with me
the thick timely thunder living in a baby's coo,
    the mysterious motion made by a fluttering wing,
    the astonishing song sounding from a morning dove.

Watch with me
a satisfaction strongly surging in a hungry heart,
    a bark beautifully bouncing from an affectionate pup,
    a soul-struck-silence blowing from a sacred spot.

"Watch with me and sing." Says the one who enables me.

A Sea Gull's Story

Early in the morning and
Through the mist gray,
Looking for me
I hear the singing sun's rays.

Sitting on the mast
Of the tired boat hurt.
Time it is for me and
My gray wings to perch.

Today, a seasoned captain bids
The sail boat, "Come to my place,
I have the perfect site
And will take you to novel heights."

In the craftsman's shop
There lives a lantern's haze.
Through his welcoming window
I peer and see the wreck afraid.

Day after day
The window whispers "watch with me."
"Look, the sail's reseamed and
Hull patched and pleased."

Continued

Somehow the old wreck sings
And begins, "I'm free."
Notes meant for the winter winds
And the captain's retreat at sea.

Dignity gentle and
Hope newly found
Spring from the captain's place,
A lovely sound in a snowy town.

My feathered wintered wings clap
At the sudden satiable sight,
For what was the old sail
Will begin a watery wonderful flight.

Adventure and love await
The boat and his crew
While I, a sea gull,
Rest wings on the mast anew.

Little Eyes in the Pizza Parlor

Entering the pizza parlor
I looked around to see.

Suddenly, I felt my finger seized
by a little hand, confidence at ease.

Grinned at me little blue eyes did,
Wasn't more than three.

Seemed like blue eyes wanted to meet
though strangers we were to be.

Innocence and passion were a masterful team,
caused me to consider how long this would be.

Would blue eyes someday make choices to be free
or miss the choices, refusing to see?

Would he make pleasure explain her tease
or choose not to choose, causing blue eyes to freeze?

I hope little eyes will tell of tranquil seas
matching the deepest blue, putting heaven at ease.

The Love of Reading

Playful shadows on the mantle and wall,
A flicker rises from its tomb, more than a crawl,
Luminosity twirls in the room, dark withdraws.

Symbols tiny become living with feel,
Lines and spaces grace with strength then zeal,
Images alive enter with the wind, so still.

A gentle read becomes ready, no stall,
Tender letters stand straight and call,
Eager pages turn and easily fall.

How will she weakened not fall but rise?
Candles light the hall and subtle lies,
Deep words warm the retreating cold, then the hungry eye.

Her heart dances with newfound friends,
Night is steady after a day's impersonal brawl.
A flame reaching high unwilling to end.

Words bathe and caress in this tempestuous world,
Words bathe and caress offering mysterious pearls.

A Violin's Christmas

Waiting I am to bring divine elegance,
        My music, tonight, magical Christmas Eve.
        Looking around, eagerness is felt,
Hearing hundreds gathered this winter eve.

Delicate flute, robust French horn,
        Sobering cello, even thunderous kettle drums;
        All scattered throughout the orchestra,
Soon to be my friends in tune and rhythm.

Nervous, courage, fright, passion
        In my harmonious strings they do swirl.
        Placed against cheek, skilled fingers I sense.
Awaiting musical magic Christmas inspiration comes.

Whether a vision real or surreal I do not know,
        The angel plays me on the first Christmas Day.
        A musical tune the heavenly baby smiles
Enlarging my heart and sweetening my strings.

For the many this night, I sweetly begin to play.
        Soar like never before my wedded strings.
        But eternal love how can I faithfully play?
Only if I hear my Maker's song amongst the throng.

Continued

Note after note, upward they twirl, rhythmic stars,
Angelic sound, troubled hearts comforted.
Something more, something more must there be
Since watching their faces heaven I can see.

Note after note ears longingly await,
Silent night, holy night is sweetly felt.
Note after note hearts warmly delight,
While I, the violin, relish this most magical of nights.

Arranging Colors

So enjoy watching the colors feed.
Springtime, rain, storm, or shine
These colors sail on the open air.

Blue, yellow, red to see, making woes think
Feather rainbows. Anticipation each day
To see what arrangement of color will be.

Red is so shy, gray knows how to coo,
Blue stands so sure, yellow is quite a lover too,
And black comes with all his pack and zoo.

Flight comes with ease, so many directions.
It's amazing they can find my place,
So much grace.

Makes me consider and think,
"Somebody knows their colors."

Gray Laughs at the Wilt

Wife's friend, husband's song,
    Child who bonds;
They no longer belong.

Gray moves to grasp,
    Tires with its gray slap,
Able to drain immortal sap.

Gray laughs at the wilt,
    Applauds the gnawing guilt,
Enjoys your agony's quilt.

Gray births miscarriages,
    Undermines good as a great beverage.
Beauty loses her humane leverage.

Truth becomes cruel,
    A false tool,
Carefully brutal.

Love moves about lame,
    Always the same,
Can't shake the killing cane.

Continued

To get what's there,
        Gray craftily shares,
Ruin is its demonic prayer.

Gray loves to entertain,
        As long as it gets to pain,
Something intensely vain.

Careful, this is no game,
        Gray would steal your flame,
Losing your divinely given aim.

Is Sand a Beauty or a Cause to Cry?

Lagoon's bottom, color all sides,
Perfect place, the sand to lie.

Beach serenade, water to grain,
Moonlit romance, no tears, no pain.

Ocean in motion, sea gulls at play,
Sandy snow, dances night and day.

Desert radiant, flowers surprise,
Wonderful to behold, my thirsty eyes.

Yet in eyes so red, pain, dismayed,
No place for sand to bed and stay.

Sand is a beauty, or a cause to cry,
Sand a plenty, looks for a place to reside.

Beauty the same, joy or pain,
Love or hate, tame or insane.

Ghosts and Their Egos

What is it that turns the TV screen
into a personal Halloween
causing healthy citizens to scream?

Ghosts and goblins are they
with their costumes of chains
and paint for the day.

Some deliver beauty,
some deliver expertise,
others divine authority.

Unaware they seem to be,
their role to haunt the TV set,
with an unseen mental threat.

What makes the birds stare with hesitation,
disgusted at the human salivation
over celebrity celebration?

What causes the moon to dim as they troll?
Only a haunting of dark souls
who lead the way with their gross egos.

Feeling Comes to the Aid of Feeling

From murkiness, stardust, mystery of space,
emerged a life, a beauty,
heaven's violin, a special face.

As the universe welcomed the moment special,
time paused, light cheered,
angelic presence presided.

In the cradle's sincerity,
new life could be heard,
attention focused on tender clarity.

Passionate child, friendly smile,
a kiss sent from heaven;
she always stayed awhile.

From under a rock, beneath the day,
Darkness came
to quiet smile's way.

Amidst the night she maintains her name,
feeling comes to aid feeling,
though it rains for countless days.

Continued

Backward stepped cold,
on the day of her birthday,
a young heart amidst those who fold.

She steps upon a sunbeam's trail,
feeling comes to the aid of feeling,
the fog she does dispel.

Elizabeth City

The sun warm reappeared after a week cold
of clouds, rain, plain, even lame.
Myself, did I find a lovely lady young
and a handsome man gentle, conversing
in the park. Elizabeth was her name;
his name I did not know, but the two were
for each other made upon the morning dew.
Many children had she; provided did he
moments so beautiful, joy played, peace enthused
even excitement relieved. Yes, so in love they seemed
both Elizabeth and he. Made for each other
they had to be; joined so perfectly you could say
like land and sea, ground and tree, warmth and breeze.
At the park her children did play,
feeding their feathered friends
on a wonderful spring day, absent of dark.
Watched sea gulls dancing, trees ever blooming,
cut grass smelling freshly did the innocent couple.
Such joy did they give me today at the park,
knowing for each other they'd been made.
Had to move away just to hear what they did say.
Now smile I can, because
Divine Wisdom had his way.
Singing is what I felt, so warmly
on this most wonderful of days.

Continued

"Awake, Awake, Awake,"
is what this couple wanted to say.
"You see, we were made for each other"
the young lady gently uttered.
Yielded my wintered heart to this
spring time affection, my heart fluttered.
So fascinated was I, I approached Elizabeth and he.
Asked could their names complete
give me over a cup of tea.
She said, "I'll be happy to sir,
it's a most wonderful treat,
my first name's Elizabeth, last name's City."

Said the young man with a grin,
"Just call me Elizabeth City's River
and her very tender friend."

The Busyness of Failed Desires

Laughter, Laughter, Laughter?
        In their hearts
                rhythm is no more.
Crying, Crying, Crying?
        Pained how desires failed
                surfaced so torn.

Lusting, Lusting, Lusting?
        Sterility wrecks
                both lovers to war.
Loving, Loving, Loving?
        Why does the
                lover's mate burn cold like a whore?

Singing, Singing, Singing?
        Notes delude young
                as their elders snore.
Thinking, Thinking, Thinking?
        Reason hopeful
                withers to no longer soar.

Wasteland, Wasteland, Wasteland!
        Failed desires spread
        through altar and gavel with a roar.

Failed Desires and a Simple Hole

On her spirited bike,
She returned with his water,
To the man wounded in mental war.

Injured, exposed, terribly aware,
He grew weak and wearied,
Dark artillery continued to mock and scar.

She grabbed her bucket's sum.
After a day's tense ride,
To the ground the bucket plunged.

Her bucket failed its sincere attempt,
No water, no gift, a deathly sum,
A simple hole relinquished the water sent.

Shocked, dismayed and mystified,
The young man sadly muttered,
"My desire, it could not satisfy."

"I will lose my candle's flame,"
His eyes began to flutter,
"The bucket wasn't its name."

Desire would've been a great tale,
A little hole got its way,
No one will prevail while hearts fail.

A Presence, I Did See

I walked the yard and in back I did see,
a simple star watching softly from tree top tall.
Watching out over the sun still water,
I saw a ripple slow, it glowed, an angel's tear flowed.
Riding down the sandy road for a moment's thrill,
I felt a windy wing nudge my automobile.
Sitting on my peaceful porch on a moonlit night,
I heard a lovely voice saying,
“Isn't that a sincere sight?"
Kissing my wife's hair,
I could smell in the fragrant air,
a lovely and most sincere prayer.
Facing life's dangers a sturdy star's wing I felt,
lovingly surround, regardless of hell's hounds,
saying, “Beware, prepare, I'm there."

Silent Thunder on the River Sweet

Did not know sat silent thunder there. . .

While fishing on lush banks of the river sweet,
I saw a butterfly resting by waters still.
Magnificent, poised, even sweetly aware,
Among fragrances abundant since roses fair.

Wings of silk tapestry near waters alive,
Breathing, shimmering, simply causing a sigh.
Visual thrill he was, butterswirl, portrait on high,
Able to stop the tears in my eyes.

The one who shared a history with the wind,
Finality surprised, heaven winged.
Anticipated flight, you colorful blend,
Surprised you wanted to be my friend.

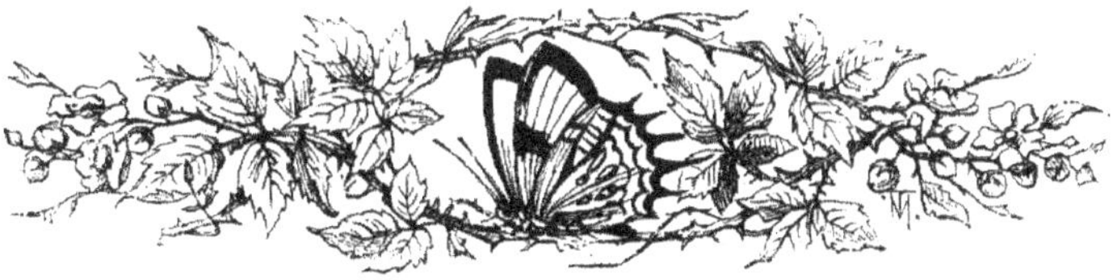

Sea Gates That Kept Her Away

From a distance, she watched waves
Come one by one.
Their sound and delight
Create such spectacular sight.

With all this beauty,
Why did her mind
Not see other times
And their potential finds?

Why did she miss the charm
Of the future find?
Sightless and tightness
In a world whispering aliveness.

Opportunity abounds
In this land profound,
But she couldn't see it
Using sight and sound.

Keeping her from the breeze,
Were gates near the glistening seas,
Yet to the closed gates
Divine poetry brought keys.

Continued

New finds occurring of all kinds;
Many have lost their stirring lines.
Happy to discover such future finds
In these awkward and peculiar times.

In a moment, they'll meet,
Her mind and find.
At last, they will speak,
With a gentle rhyme.

To Make Him Smile

A little boy composed a prayer I heard,
In the midst of a rambunctious herd,
He said a most thirsty word.

"I only want
To make you smile.
    When darkness gets in my way,
    It's such a sad, sad day.
I want you to hold
My hand this hour.
    Because you are the one
    With the most beautiful smile."

Mama then prayed
A most fascinating word
While her little boy listened without a stir.

"Time sings to you
For only an eternal while.
    Space for you dances
    Amidst the eyes of my child.
For you to approvingly smile,
My heart suddenly aspires.
    Whenever I am in the midst
    Of the whirl gone wild,
Please help my desire
To make you and my child eternally smile."

Searching for Stars

Hungry soul, where did you
        diligently swim
to find your heart's ease
        and begin again?

You searched
        so many nights
to see distant and
        peaceful lights.

Comforted
        from afar
did angels
        and simple stars.

Couldn't you feel
        In their wings there's no gray?
"Certainly"
        you will say.

Daybreak sublime
        lit their way,
surrounded by a world
        lost in gray.

Continued

For still seas
    did you long,
from an East breeze
    a gentle song.

Who
    can you trust
and not
    diligently blush?

Crossed your path
    that day did he,
wonderfully
    on your way toward we.

Materialistic fever
    subdued for thee,
discovering a
    mental refuge by his sea.

Wounds he tended
    through creative steady jots,
such splendid divine poetry
    came from a favorite divine spot.

To Play or Not to Play

Though adult desires
    carelessly swirl,
    fluttering corn husks
joyously unfurl.

Today and tomorrow
    the chaotic evolves,
    yet colored leaves many
twirling fall.

As decayed intuition
    cautiously crawls,
    swaying pines stand
royal and tall.

Human creativity
    slavishly dribbles,
    yet red berries
freely jiggle.

Sophistication stiff
    encourages the fog,
    but clapping leaves
laugh and applaud.

Continued

Many fads
mostly succumb that day,
while wind swept grasses
honestly play.

Egos darkened
slide beneath the song,
though feathered songs
gently glide along.

Human imagination
violently gets stoked,
while a chimney's smoke
drifts unprovoked.

Blinding pride burns
inside the human book,
as a camp side fire
rises to have a good look.

Memories of a Brownie

The perfect little size
hidden from all the family spies,
    leaves just enough crumbs
    so you can say, "I'm not done."
It melts in your mouth,
let there be no doubt.
    Brown and chewy,
    but not too gooey.
Just enough flake
and rarely over baked.
    Brownies today are not far away
    as the home missed today by the bay.

Where is the Sacredness?

Can you hear
the whisper in the air,
almost a certain
sacredness everywhere?

Can you feel
the otherworldly chimes
in the midst
of these gentle rhymes?

The little town sleeps
with open eyes
and few
can hear poetic cries.

The routine
has successfully denied,
the heart
the opportunity to sigh.

Look to the Artist
and his poetic sky
amidst
the incoming tide.

Sweet Tea (We)

A time before,
    It used to be you and me.
    Large felt the world,
Truly lonely, and lengthy.

As a hollow theme
    Did you feel me.
    Before we were a seam,
You couldn't hear me.

In a world killing
    Many a lovers' dream,
    We hasn't come so easily.
But with a new song, you and I are we.

You and I presented the world flashes of we,
    And some mindful moments
    Of just thee and me.
Gradually, we learned to feel and be.

At times, there's a place
    For just silly you and silly me,
    Because it took you and me
To make our significant we.

Continued

You and I searched for
    That higher place called, "we";
    A place we learned how to feel
At tender ease, youthful and free.

Love you I do,
    From that higher grace, I embrace thee.
    Love me you do,
While your heart learns to breathe.

Now, we're like the playful we
Of tasty sugar and delicious tea.

Puppy

Who keeps Mama safe and sound
when Daddy's not around?
Puppy little with his
persistent trumpet sound.

Who keeps cats away when they stray
too close to flowers in the morning hours?
Puppy little with his quick feet and heart beat
thumping a million miles an hour.

Who let's Mama know
when Daddy's coming home?
Puppy little looking for his vittles' home
and maybe even a milky bone.

Puppy little who's really three
looks out for you and me.
Part of the family destined is he,
catching Frisbees so successfully.

Adoring he's learned to be,
all this and only three.

Connoisseur of Pleasure

Dad, to pleasure's hour,
who knows its secret power?
Where the delicious red apple dwells
who can guide in such an entangled hell?

Here a power enchants, my eyes in a trance,
my heart hears no other dance.
Through the sensual haze where is the wise one
who can show me the way?

My son, pleasure wears many faces;
a connoisseur of pleasure you must embrace.
Not the same worth is all wine,
for every thirsty time.

Not all pleasures are worth
a moment's birth on this tender earth.
So Dad, who is the connoisseur
That can save me from the flaming skewer?

Lad, heavenly joy loved by a disciplined heart
can see each face of pleasure's spark.
Some faces lead to anger, confusion some, others free
make the heart sing in a bouquet of worthy dreams.

Continued

Pleasure needs her tasteful guide,
        or no one will survive.
A heart disciplined discernibly knocks
        and enters heaven's rapturous spot.

There, pleasure is a secret power,
        hungered for by a world gone sour.
It sounds like you, Dad, have sight
        as a connoisseur of unusual delight.

Amidst the sensual song in the night
        you stand where few souls can stand the fight.
Son, I discover my pleasure with a rose,
        a rose that shares her pleasure with me.

We, a perceiving and fruitful blend
        get caught up in heaven's revealing wind.
Your mother, my most pleasing find,
        I consider my most marvelous vine.

Worthy pleasures are divinely supplied,
        with a dedicated heart we share all kinds.
Dad, I cannot sip and drink this power,
        I'm too young, it's before my timely hour.

Continued

Son, I know this is not your hour
because learn you must to pursue heaven's flower.
Oh please, do not become like all who sour,
caught up in pleasure's entangling power.

Unless a connoisseur of pleasure you become,
you'll never know heaven's spectacular hours.

Heaven Entrusted Her to Me

A little fawn she was;
Heaven entrusted her to me.
Bruised, hungry, tender was she
While running through the field of dense mortality.
Wounded she lay with only heaven to say
What could be done as the fawn lay in the hay.
From death and indifference, eager eyes looked on
Cackling at the ease of catching their belly's calm.
Salivating over the vulnerable fawn,
Didn't know fierce angels looked on.
Along came a young boy who happened to be at play,
Saw the little fawn laying in the hay on that day.
The young child looked down and excited he was to find
Heaven's lonely fawn in a place he would be.
With heaven's love looking over them at dawn
The young lad escaped with his speckled little fawn.
The two grew up with angels looking on
Remembering the day, an angel's prayer, discovered the fawn.
Amazingly to me a young man I became
And heaven's little life became a woman and heaven's glee.

The Sounds of Summer

Morning doves coo,
Simple notes heard, symphonic glee.
Whispers poetic atop springtime trees,
Singing, singing, windy notes, freely, freely.

Evening frogs duet together,
Summer rains shower souls sublime.
Whispers in the field, poetic sounds and flowers divine,
Worshiping, celestial tune, all belong, song after song.

Winged violins fervently play
Poetic sonatas this very day.
Pulsing stars, cadence belongs,
Desiring and joining Earth's chorus from afar.

Summer rains drip, drip, drip even tip, tip, tip.
Eyes sleep deep so whispers twirl for both boy and girl.
Effortless rhythms swirl through the chimney drum,
Anticipating poetic joy for older hearts young.

Song birds appear, orchestra practice near,
Grandma cheers for beauty and no fear.
Lifting cantatas are tenderly perched;
Their hearts a singin', "No fear; poetic whispers search."

Continued

Poetic feelings, desires otherworldly,
Beyond the ordinary and mental sedentary.
Whether spring, summer, winter, or fall;
Taste poetic whispers both large and small.

Pleasure, oh pleasure; surprise, surprise;
If merely a world with no plan or design.
Both love and beauty ingeniously pursue,
Astonished Deity's pleasure could surely renew.

Cruel Felines

Earthly beauties many,
So few with untainted hearts.
Anything for money goes,
Fame and glamorous pictures, oh no!
It seems like such an infinite regress,
Too many ladies continually fail the test.
Try to get close to such a case,
You'll wish you had another face.
Divine wisdom caught me on that day,
Planning me for another she on the way.
A she who drank from different waters near
The well of sincerity, what a lovely, tender thrill.
A higher place sweet where tender souls meet
Having fallen from their heart and well balanced feet.
Some ladies want their revenge,
Knowing another kind put them far behind.
They know they're not the sweetest wine
Just a spear to ruin someone's heart and keep it blind.
So, sincerity must show its vigor and best
In moments where felines hunt their quest.
I'm sorry if you chose to not be your best,
I'm so glad I chose she, sincerity.
Because I'd be like all the rest
Having failed a major human test.

Family Should be a Higher Place

A higher place where minds are birthed,

Hearts learn to
feel their worth,
Conscience begins
to thrive on earth.

Father and mother their vision share,

Sister and brother
learn to share,
Family and pets
become friends there.

A place where bodies learn to run for fun,

Souls begin to sing
in prayer to the One,
Desire begins its quest
for beauty's sum.

Continued

Love becomes divinely defined before the age of nine,

Strength softly moves

these little feet from the vastly deep,

Gentleness firmly guides

the human cry until eyes dry.

Wisdom looked and said, "This is good."
Wisdom looked and said, "This is good."

To Wife, My Love

Beautiful then,
　　Beautiful now;
Time graces her
　　With a heart divine.

Winter then,
　　Winter now;
Heavenly warmth
　　Inflames and sustains her.

Labor then,
　　Labor now;
Rest looks on
　　Wanting to soothe her.

Breath then,
　　Breath now;
Life much easier
　　When breathing heaven's pine.

Husband

Plundered, She Weeps

Plunder deep her soul as she weeps,
Lied she did not, but he did lie.
    It meant nothing to see love sigh,
    He didn't care it crucified.

She did not know such grief so deep
Could come from his smiles wonderfully sweet.
    Nail after nail brings tear after tear,
    He must know her heart violently seared.

Looked into his heart she really peeked
To find a cave dark where shadows creep.
    Lied she did not, but he did lie,
    He didn't care love crucified.

He would not feel, he could not feel
Her love a treasure in a world full of eels.
    Plunder deep her soul as she weeps,
    You dark cave where shadows creep.

If she opens the curtain,
New light emerges certain.
    Honesty's warmth is what she'll feel,
    No more dark shadows that craftily steal.

My Favorite Tree

I know there is a smile in thee,
        Something a boss might not see
In a company employee.

I know there is a smile in thee,
        Something a Master poet sees
In a world of desperate pleas.

I know there is a smile in thee,
        Something your man will need
Like a bird resting in his favorite tree.

The Lover's Call

Now with the poet's ear
    is heard the Lover's call,
nowhere more needed
    near a word's nightfall.
Musical seeds need
    the touch of uplifting hands,
in situations where the dead
    constantly countermand.

On the human boulevard
    is heard the wreckage of words,
crashed and burned
    smashed and upturned.
Stagnate language greets with
    no warmth or kindly rhythm,
becomes a place devoted
    to lifeless algorithms.

Tongues are drunk
    with constant confusion,
destroy the romance
    of a faithful fusion.
    Manners look
for a loyal friend,
    a place to call home
as courtesy ends.

Continued

Honest eyes seduced
by intimacy's discomposure,
it used to be
an innocent exclosure.
Foul minds that be
no longer know their hearts,
a wearisome place
for love to start.

With the poet's pen
I write for thee,
wanting a heart dull
to graciously begin.
Longing to produce
a non-secular sound,
coldness from a
false-hearted age glumly surrounds.

Scorched places will see again
the human daffodil,
refreshing the withered
land like a timely watermill.
On your spring day
a celestial harmony that trills,
will cut through
the noise and clutter that chills.

Continued

Within my heart chambers
deep channels intertwine,
hungry to write
a note especially divine.
For all my many days
a desire gentle flows,
deep within the poet's abode
a concerto grows.

Beauty and pain
knock at human strongholds,
virtuous sights rest still
desiring to be told.
To set them free,
to sing, to play, to uplift,
to love, to reveal,
this is the poet's gift.

I am surprised Poetry
formed me sublime,
blended together
these strings of mine.
The expressions of the Poet
caress a sea of daffodils,
as they stroll up and down
field after field after field.

Biting Frost

I observed an encounter between
A grown man who needed love's theme
And a small dog displaying love's gleam.

Later, in the chilly night, the puppy's warm nod
Was met with, "Hey you, bad dog, bad dog."
How can anyone be enthused over such smog?

He aimed to put out the dog's "glad to see ya" like a Grinch.
He launched stiff arrows that served to singe and pinch.
But, maturity found a home in the dog that didn't flinch.

Tonight, I learned the man's aim.
Biting frost is his deadly game.
"Winter" is his chosen name.

A Mother Cat Speaks

Early in the morning,
dew on the ground,
a sliver of moon,
crows call in the background.

A silent night,
my work is done,
in a place of light,
I've left my little one.

He purrs with a message,
on the lawn mower he lays,
waiting for the selected soul,
my little kitten I trade.

Knowing a lyrical letter
is about to grace this day,
from the woods I hear,
a needy song, he's afraid.

Though I hear him cry
I cannot purr his lullaby,
but in my kitten's eye,
soon, handsome laughter will reside.

Continued

Open, the door surges,
heaven's target quickly emerges,
he comes to the needy sound,
lying near the grassy ground.

Surprise, Surprise!
I see in this human eye,
a tender plan in merciful motion
begins a heart's soothing lotion.

Beautiful eyes,
little feet,
needy sounds,
all vulnerably greet.

Today is the day,
a kitten will want to play,
there's an arising twinkle in his eye
just like the Messenger on High.

Listening to a Whistling Train

Between the whistling train and the wind at midnight,
    I heard their pleasant conversation take flight,
    Without a hint the train whistled an honest plea,
Blowing and flowing in the summer's breeze.

Both the train and wind agreed,
    So these gentle questions they sent me.
    How will weak words ascend without wings?
How do embers rise without a lifting breeze?

Don't you know gentle embers do call to thee?
    Write them down carefully, for us three.
    Together they granted me a calm-cool night,
A wonder needed to rid the gibberish blight.

A persuasive place filled with the moon's song-light,
Sounds to wash away noises and nagging fright.

Your Voice Tells Me

Your voice tells me that the day is good,
          That the love is there,
With future memories to share.

Sets like the glorious moon at bed time,
          Your voice rises like the sun to sing,
And dances when freedom rings.

While the birds rest in tender sleep,
          Your voice rests for the day's new wheat,
Given by love's amazing paraclete.

Your voice halts the world's mental madness,
          A sound that hungers to resist the sadness,
And thirsts for the best from heaven's gladness.

Touches my soul with an uncanny earnestness,
          Your voice soothes the jungle's ugliness,
And tenderly stirs with a God-given fearlessness.

No other voice sounds with your sound as you pray,
          Or captures melody your radiant way,
Or says what you say, especially this day.

Half-a-Juliet

Lifeless walk, woman submersed,
Alcohol inspired, dying of thirst.
Stars unseen through her blurry windows,
She gave up on Eve some time ago.

She's a tree without limbs, a dastardly plan,
the beetles chew on her wedding band.
Words hard to find on trees cold and frail
She's a broken poem, emotions misspelled.

Disheveled spirit, arousal denied,
No spirited arteries as her heart clots defy.
She's no place for a heart to bountifully breathe,
There's no innocent move from femininity.

Festivity declines, her notes do strain,
Half-a-Juliet comes from ghoulish ways.
Her story filled constantly with war,
The songbird won't sing for her anymore.

She thirsts for afternoons with sun and sand,
some place to lay her head and hand.
Her gloom needs some cheerful places,
Anxious and stiff, a mannequin on display.

Continued

A hero she needs from another land,

        A hero she needs more than mere man.

        An artist from Nazareth, a beautifying vision,

Fills Eve's heart and becomes a woman lifted.

She will have good days,

        in a place of war.

        She will have good days,

while Aslan roars.

NOTES

NOTES

NOTES

NOTES

NOTES

NOTES

NOTES

NOTES

NOTES

NOTES

NOTES

www.ingramcontent.com/pod-product-compliance
Lightning Source LLC
Chambersburg PA
CBHW020020050426
42450CB00005B/558
9780615134680